Treasure

Mythology

Step Inside The Fascinating World Of Greek Gods, Heroes, Monsters, And Other Mythical Creatures

Austin D. Kaplan

Bluesource And Friends

This book is brought to you by Bluesource And Friends, a happy book publishing company.

Our motto is **"Happiness Within Pages"**

We promise to deliver amazing value to readers with our books.

We also appreciate honest book reviews from our readers.

Connect with us on our Facebook page www.facebook.com/bluesourceandfriends and stay tuned to our latest book promotions and free giveaways.

Don't forget to claim your FREE books!

Brain Teasers:

https://tinyurl.com/karenbrainteasers

Harry Potter Trivia:
https://tinyurl.com/wizardworldtrivia
Sherlock Puzzle Book (Volume 2)

https://tinyurl.com/Sherlockpuzzlebook2

Also check out our other books

"67 Lateral Thinking Puzzles"

https://tinyurl.com/thinkingandriddles

"Rookstorm Online Saga"

https://tinyurl.com/rookstorm

"Korman's Prayer"

https://tinyurl.com/kormanprayer

"The Convergence"

https://tinyurl.com/bloodcavefiction

"The Hardest Sudokos In Existence
(Ranked As The Hardest Sudoku Collection
Available In The Western World)"

https://tinyurl.com/MasakiSudoku

thus be thought of as universal. As befitting its nature, it is presented without assurance regarding its prolonged validity or interim quality. Trademarks that are mentioned are done without written consent, and can in no way be considered an endorsement from the trademark holder.

Description

Enter a world where gods and goddesses mingle with the humans that worship them in elaborate temples, where heroes fight epic battles and monsters are thwarted, where legendary tales are told with an eye toward eternal glory: The treasure that is Greek mythology is an undeniable pleasure to read. Explore another world of ancient values, virtues, and vices— never to be forgotten.

The motifs of Greek mythology are similar to that of many other mythologies: Supernatural power is a handy way to explain the extraordinary; heroes are larger-than-life, with superhuman strength and wisdom to spare; gods are tricky and should be approached with caution; harrowing journeys are undertaken; battles are fought, and champions are forged. The Greeks developed a highly sophisticated government and developed both the Western epic and the philosophical tradition; their influence is undeniable still yet today. We can see the Greek evolution from their legendary founding, to their epic expansion, to their continued presence in our popular imagination through the thread of their treasure trove of myths and tales.

This book can take you through that journey, beginning with an overview of the Greek peoples and cultures, and into an understanding of their pantheon of gods and goddesses, their amazing tales of adventure, restless search for meaning, and a glimpse into who they actually were via the stories they held dear. Some specific elements you will encounter include:

- Some of the main gods of the Greco-Roman pantheon, with all their quirks and foibles
- The Greek Council of Twelve Gods and their all-too-human role in the peoples they oversee
- The first epic tales that have defined Western literary culture for thousands of years

- The multiple myths surrounding the gods, their heroes, and their foes

- The unique philosophy and government of ancient Greece, which created the foundation for all of the Western civilization

- From the Minotaur to Medusa to the Cyclops—fascinating creatures fueling mythological tales

- Stories about some of the most legendary figures in mythological history: Theseus and Perseus

- Contemporary visions of Greek characters and how they inform our Western institutions, our literary and artistic history, and our contemporary culture

Roman mythology is diverse and fascinating, offering us an insight into how ancient people believed and lived, into what they valued and vilified, and into how they lived and thrived. Finally, if you have enjoyed these treasured tales of Greek mythology, don't forget to explore the other fantastic realms of mythological magic in this series of books: *Treasures of Egyptian Mythology, Treasures of Celtic Mythology, Treasures of Norse Mythology,* and *Treasures of Roman Mythology.* You will find yourself in awe of the sweeping scope of history and culture represented by these mythological traditions—as well as get a better understanding of how we continually make and re-make these myths for our own times. That's the fabulous thing about myths: They never truly die.

Introduction

Undoubtedly, the Greeks loom large in the popular as well as the historical imagination. From *Clash of the Titans*, its remake, to *300*, and its sequel, popular culture has made entertaining use of Greek mythology. The real history and mythology, as it turns out, is even more fascinating than the film and television interpretations. It is hard to say, definitively, who the Greek people were, especially as their influence grew: Many peoples of many different cultures ultimately absorbed the historical, mythological, and philosophical ideas of this foundational Western culture. Still, there are certain elements of Greek culture that remain distinctly Greek, and its legacy is undeniably present.

The motifs of Greek mythology, in general, are similar to that of many other mythologies: Magic is a handy way to explain the extraordinary; heroes are larger-than-life, with strength and wisdom to spare; gods are tricky and should be approached with caution; harrowing journeys are undertaken; battles are fought, and warriors are forged. There is always the constant reminder of the fragility of life, in the fear over land and harvest, destiny and fate. Loyalty, bravery, and sacrifice are tantamount; there is also a hefty dose of wit and wisdom, the chicanery needed to fool the gods or deceive an enemy, and the smarts to know how best to hold on to land and power. Not to mention the unquenching thirst for adventure, and the desire to achieve everlasting glory.

From the Olympian pantheon of deities, to the substantial and lasting impact of the Greco-Roman tradition, Greek mythology offers an array of exciting adventure, heroic exploits, and time-honored tales. So, embark upon these stories with the Athenian spirit—the birthplace of Western philosophy and democracy. Gathered herein are the many complex, but still commonplace, mythological stories out of the cradle of Western civilization.

Chapter 1:
An Overview of the Greek Peoples and Cultures

The influence of Greek history, culture, and government are found everywhere in contemporary Western society, not to mention its popular inspiration on entertainment. But what were the Greek people like, and where do they come from? Truly, Greece is the veritable birthplace of Western civilization—the source for philosophy, literature, drama, history, mathematics, and democracy. This amazing amalgamation of islands created a cultural explosion of ideas that would resonate throughout history, from about 2500 BCE until the current day.

Located in southeastern Europe, Greece is comprised of many islands, including Crete and the Cyclades, jutting off from its peninsular mainland. This geography meant that the Greek peoples were a seafaring lot—their livelihoods depended on the moods of the Mediterranean; hence, a lot of their eventual mythology and literature deal directly with the sea on which it depended. This also meant that Greek fishermen became explorers and then conquerors, settling on coastal regions elsewhere. Unlike the Romans, they did not go on to conquer vast swathes of territory, but the size of their influence—passed along subsequently through the Romans—belies the size of their nation-state.

When referring to ancient Greece and its peoples, the term "Hellenistic" is often used. This is not, as is often thought, derived from the myth of Helen of Troy recounted in *The Iliad* and other stories. Rather, it comes from the foundational myth of Greece itself: As in Biblical stories, the ancient Greek mythology held that there was a great flood that wiped out most of humanity. The mythical Deucalion and Pyrrha repopulated the land by casting stones into the receding waters; the first to spring into life was Hellen. He and his sons not only repopulated the land, but became the first powerful family to rule throughout. Thus, the term "Hellenes" was used to describe the people, and "Hellenistic", to describe the culture.

Because the history of Greece is so long and fascinating, scholars often divide it into periods, including the Cycladic and Minoan, to the Mycenaean and Classical. The Cycladic and Minoan periods overlap somewhat, as the former describes a group of people who settled on the Aegean islands, while the latter describes a group that settled on and around Crete. These periods marked the building of temples—thus, the beginning of mythological worship—and the advent of the seafaring trade. The Minoans also developed a system of writing—thus, the beginnings of a great civilization had begun. It is generally agreed that the Minoans overtook the Cycladic peoples, then themselves fell to the Mycenaeans after the devastating eruption of a nearby volcano.

The later Mycenaean period (circa 1900-1100 BCE) saw the further establishment of culture with sophisticated architectural achievements, the development of writing, and the refinement of the pantheon of gods that would eventually become the Olympians we know of today. The cause of the fall of the Mycenaean peoples around 1100 BCE is unknown, but it is from them that Homer got the tale of the fall of Troy for his great epic, *The Iliad*. For about three hundred years after that, there is no written record from the Greeks, though there is evidence of expansion throughout Asia Minor. Between the 8th and 7th centuries BCE, Homer is writing not only *The Iliad*, but also *The Odyssey*—the two foundational texts of the whole of Western literature—and the beginnings of democracy were being established throughout Greece. With "demos" meaning state, and "Kratos" meaning people, the state of and by the people was the most astounding innovation in government in the history of the Western world. The organized city-state governed by consistent laws would be, perhaps, the greatest legacy of ancient Greece.

Because of Greece's terrain—mountainous regions and singular islands—the nation, as we know it today, was never completely unified in ancient times. Instead, it was a grouping of city-states, wherein shared cultural influences, such as religion and language, created a loose unity, but each separate government had independence. Still, city-states would come together and fight against a common enemy, such as the Persians, and they created another lasting legacy which would also serve to foster common feeling: The Olympic Games.

The ancient Olympic Games were held every four years, as the modern ones are, at Olympia, a site sacred to Zeus, the king of gods. A massive sporting spectacle, Greeks and others from all over the ancient world would compete. The ancient Olympics lasted for 293 consecutive games—a record we are not even close to attaining with our modern day Olympic Games.

Other places to gather included local temples, which fostered a sense of unity and a sense of independent pride in your particular city-state. For example, the patron saint of Athens was Athena, who was important throughout Greek society, but particularly so to Athens. As well, there was the centralized marketplace, the agora, where citizens of every status could gather and trade.

Also during this time, we get Classical Greece that most of us think about when we think of Greece, between roughly 500-400 BCE. This is when Socrates, Plato, and Aristotle were inventing Western philosophy, when the Acropolis is built, and when the scientific method was introduced, and the structure of the universe began to be understood.

The Greek development in philosophical thinking is, besides democracy, its longest-lasting legacy. The emphasis on logic and reason began with the renowned Socrates, and was passed down via his student Plato, and then Plato's student, Aristotle. This kind of thinking encouraged an investigation into natural phenomena and behavior through rational engagement. It also encouraged the back-and-forth method of questioning and exploring, the so-called "Socratic dialogue" that is still used in classrooms across the world today.

The Greeks also contributed to fields of mathematics and science (and, really, at this time, philosophy was not truly distinct from science). Basic concepts such as geometry and mathematical proofs came to us through Euclid and Pythagoras—what high school geometry student hasn't bemoaned the Pythagorean proof? Hippocrates also flourished during the classical time, founding a medical school and establishing standard practices for the time. The Hippocratic Oath—first, do no harm—is still recited by doctors today.

Concerning the arts, literature also flourished during the classical age, with the importance of theatre and poetry. The playwrights, Sophocles and Aristophanes, established the conventions of the genre of theater that are still maintained today; a dialogue between the characters was, essentially, their invention. The oral tradition of reciting great events via poetic means was also significant to the Greeks, and in Homer, we have the father of all Western literature. He wrote these oral poems down by informal ways, establishing the epic conventions that define the genre. Many scholars suggest that the whole of Western literature owes a debt to either *The Iliad* or *The Odyssey* (more on those in Chapters 7 and 8).

The visual art of ancient Greece was also markedly influential, particularly in the areas of sculpture and architecture. The American Capitol building and the White House—two notable structures symbolizing power—owe debts of gratitude to the Greco-Roman style. In sculpture, the Greeks worked to encapsulate the beauty of the human form and spirit. Artists were particularly concerned with proportion, and their creations intended to represent an idealized human form. That kind of artistic ideal would be resurrected in the Renaissance, which undeniably spurred the most remarkable achievements in Western art history. In addition, Greek pottery and other vessels for everyday use have also been preserved, marking a civilization that was concerned with beauty and form in all realms of life.

The survival of ancient Greek culture and its historical and artistic achievements was due, in large part, to the Romans: Not only did the Romans adopt the Greek pantheon of gods and goddesses, along with many of their rituals and festivals, but they also borrowed from the Greek, styles of sculpture and architecture. The expansion of the Roman Empire ensured that the elements of Greek influence would also be dispersed throughout Europe, Asia, and

Northern Africa, and then, eventually, onto the New World via exploration and conquest.

The waning of classical Greece began with the internecine Peloponnesian Wars: The great power that Athens wielded over the rest of the city-states—remember, Greece is not a unified nation but a set of city-states across many regions—led to growing unrest, particularly with Sparta. Essentially, for the last fifty-plus years of the classical period, from circa 460 BCE to 404 BCE, these two ruling powers clashed. History—and contemporary popular culture—had left us with a vision of Athens as a place of ideas and philosophy, while Sparta was a place of discipline and military. Neither view is entirely correct, but perhaps, broadly speaking, there is some truth to it. In any event, the first was between the two factions that ended in a truce and a feeling of fragile peace, but the second left Athens in ruins and Sparta bankrupt. This vacuum of power paved the way for Philip II of Macedon to take power over the

Greek realm, leading to the ascension of his famed son, Alexander the Great.

Alexander the Great lived up to his name by conquering Persia (modern day Iran) and other large swathes of territory, spreading Greek culture and influence throughout what we now know as the Middle East, into Egypt, and even India. Upon Alexander's death, the empire was divided between four generals—all lesser men than the great Alexander—which weakened the central power. During this time, Rome was beginning its rapid rise to imperial status, and Greece came increasingly under the control of the Romans. By 146 BCE, Greece became a protectorate of Rome—no longer its own nation or city-state. But, even in its fall, Greece retained an unprecedented power within Rome, where its politics, fashions, philosophies—and yes, its mythologies—were continuously followed. Indeed, when most scholars refer to the founding of Western civilization and the ancient world that created it, the two cultures are intertwined under the moniker "Greco-Roman" civilization, or history or art. Still, Greece has a place of primacy—the literal cradle from which the birth of Western civilization began.

PART I: Gods and Goddesses

The pantheon of Greek gods and goddesses is derived from many ancient sources that grew into a unified religion that influenced ancient life for thousands of years. Also, the lasting popularity of these myths and figures is undeniable, given the ubiquitous presence of Greco-Roman themes and figures in many modern-day incarnations.

The gods who appear with frequency happen to be many-skilled and brave warriors, as well as clever tricksters and active participants in every day human events. One of the hallmarks of the gods and goddesses throughout Greco-Roman mythology is that they are representations of particular ideas that their respective societies held at the time—and, as such, are very human in nature. This canon of mythology is perhaps the most anthropomorphized of the popular mythological traditions. Gods and goddesses don't simply witness events from above or beyond—they are active participants in the said events, and work to manipulate the interactions of humans, and the events of human history. Also, many of the tales that introduce us to the gods and goddesses change over time to meet the society's different needs at different moments—this is true for virtually all mythological traditions.

The tales surrounding the gods and goddesses of Greek mythology—as is also common with all mythologies—are usually stories that either seek to confirm a common cultural ideal, or work to provide a cautionary function. That is, myths are told to remind us of who we are, where we come from, and attempt to preserve the goodness of a particular way of life. On the other hand, myths can be told like parables, warning us against the dangers of going against a particular value or cultural norm. When we read these tales in contemporary times, we may not always agree on the "goodness" of that way of life, because our value systems are probably different. But they still give us an insight into what heroism and triumph, or villainy and trial meant to a certain people at a certain time. As such, they are fascinating to read—and to learn from—giving us a window into an ancient culture that is so very different from our own.

The gods and goddesses of these myths are, likewise, designed either to represent an ideal to which humans should aspire—a role model of sorts—or to discourage certain types of behavior. Being anthropomorphized gods and goddesses, they can be fickle and changeable—not always to be trusted or feared. They remain figures of awe and reverence because of their supernatural gifts and abilities, regardless of their actions, and the power that they seemingly have over humans inspires us to return again and again to their marvelous stories.

CHAPTER 2:
Uranus, Cronus, and the Battle of the Titans

The father of all, Uranus (or Ouranus), came out of the primordial myths to create the universe. From Uranus came Cronus (or Kronos), and from Cronus, came Zeus—hence, we have the creation of the familiar Greek pantheon of gods. Unlike other mythological origin stories, the Greek cosmology rested on conflict and struggle; without the battles between the Titans and the Olympians, we would not have the supremacy of Zeus and the ever-meddling pantheon of Greek gods and goddesses. Greek mythology was complicated—a sophisticated set of multiple artistic explanations for the origins of the universe and the order of the world as they knew it.

In the beginning, there were four forces in the universe: Chaos, Gaia (Earth), Tartarus (Abyss), and Eros (Love). From out of Gaia comes Uranus

(Heaven), and the production process begins, with the creation of their many offspring: Among them the race of the one-eyed Cyclops, the giants, known as "Hecatoncheires", and a significant son, Cronus (Time). After Uranus' rule in the realm of the gods becomes harsh and punitive, Cronus wages war against him, encouraged by Gaia—thus establishing a long and well-used trope in Western literature—that of the son usurping the father. The myth suggests that Cronus, in fact, castrated his father with a scythe given to him by his mother; one need not look far to find echoes throughout Western literature (the Oedipus story, for one).

However, this very act of rebellion leads Cronus to also fear his own children, along with a prophecy that encourages his fear of usurpation. Thus, Cronus begins to eat his own children, ensuring that none shall someday overthrow him. Only Zeus was to escape this fate when his mother Rhea gave Cronus a

stone swaddled in clothing to swallow instead of
Zeus.

Indeed, Zeus would have his revenge after he is
grown, conquering his father and forcing him to spit
up all his other siblings; once again, the son usurps
the father. In the story of Zeus' conquest, however, it
goes further: Not only does Zeus overthrow his
father's reign, but he defeats the entire pantheon of
Titans.

The Titans were the proto-gods in Greek
mythology—the twelve children of Gaia and
Uranus—who bore the gods, some of whom would
eventually become gods and goddesses alongside
Zeus and his siblings. Others would be classified as
"Titans". The Titans were, in fact, characterized by
their struggle against whatever might come their way;
they were not the originators of order, but rather, the
early prototypes against which the Olympians would
come to be seen. Thus, their defeat was inevitable if

an order was to be maintained in the universe. Zeus and his cohort of siblings were able to defeat them, after ten long years of battle, and banished them all to Tartarus—much deeper in the underworld than even Hades. Only then could Zeus take up the mantle of the father of the Olympians and create a peaceful order under which humankind would flourish. The twelve Titans then give way to the twelve Olympians and other assorted minor deities.

Another part of the Greek origin story is that of the hero: The great heroes of Greek mythology are all born of the merging of the gods with the mortals, thus melding the two worlds. These heroes are the epitome of the best that humankind has to offer, and their great exploits elevate a particularly desirable characteristic: For example, the twelve labors of Hercules emphasize perseverance as well as strength of body and mind, while the many years Penelope waits for Odysseus celebrates the virtues of patience and fidelity. The heroes are also credited with founding the great city-states of Greece, such as Theseus in Athens, or Perseus in Mycenae. Therefore, the lineage is passed down from the origins of the universe (Gaia and company) through the Titans and their chaotic ways, to the Olympians and their representative order, to the half-mortal humans themselves, who founded the very culture we still yet study.

Also, lest we forget, archeological discoveries made as recently as the 19th century give credence to the notion that Greek mythology is founded in some kind of reality—the discovery of the actual ruins of the actual city of Troy being perhaps the most significant. The Greeks were embellishing stories about their real historical origins, creating both a system of belief and an artistic expression of explanation, not only of history, but also of natural phenomena and human achievement.

Thus, the origin story of Greek mythology is similar to that of other mythologies in a fundamental way: It is about creating order out of chaos—the founding of a system of thought and behavior that will unify society in ways conducive to the expansion of civilization. The Titans themselves are larger-than-life characters who serve to explain natural phenomena (Atlas holding up the world, for example) and function as opposing forces to the Olympian pantheon of accepted gods. The very real—and often very flawed—Olympians would be seen as infinitely preferable to the cruel and violent Titans. Just as we define ourselves by what we emulate, we also define ourselves but what we fervently wish not to be. The Titans are excellent foils for the more ordered, more humane Olympians, who function as patrons of the heroes to which all of humankind looks to for inspiration.

CHAPTER 3:
The Many Myths of Zeus, God of Thunder

As father of the Olympians, Zeus was a terrible and awesome figure, capable of hurtling destruction down upon those who defy him, and, at the same time, be the champion of those who placate him with offerings. He walked amidst humankind with ease— indeed, he not only frequently consorted with mortals, but mated with them—and meted out justice via signs and omens. A punisher and peacemaker, Zeus occupied the top position in the pantheon, and the most important temples throughout ancient Greece.

The son of Cronus, Zeus was the only child of Cronus to escape the fate of the others—that of being eaten by their father. Zeus, instead, was hidden away to grow up strong and, ultimately, to fulfill his fate: He forces Cronus to regurgitate his other children, then, bonding with his siblings, waged war against Cronus and the other Titans to gain power. He and his cohorts sat atop Mount Olympus, and the Olympians would become the mightiest pantheon of gods in the ancient Western world.

Zeus himself was married to Hera, but was inclined to pursue extramarital adventures throughout his reign; thus, he had innumerable offspring, many of whom became some of the most notable of the Olympian gods and goddesses. He is the father of Ares, the god of war, and Apollo, the most beloved and beautiful of all the ancient gods. He is also the father of Hermes, the messenger of the gods, and Dionysius, the patron god of wine and revelry. He is the father of the doomed Persephone, imprisoned in the underworld. He is the father of the great heroes, Perseus and Hercules, of the mesmerizing Helen, who launched the Trojan War. With the Titan, Themis, Zeus is the father of the Fates, the Hours, the Seasons, Justice, and Peace: Without Zeus, there would be no

civilization. Out of all of these children, only Ares
was his child with Hera.

He is also the father to Athena—perhaps the wisest
and most resourceful of the Greek gods—and
certainly the favorite daughter of Zeus. She was born
of Zeus' little-known first wife, the Titan, Metis, and
had an improbable beginning. Zeus, fearing that the
same fate that had befallen his father would befall
him—namely, that his own son would overthrow
him—he swallowed the pregnant Metis.
Nevertheless, Athena persevered and emerged, fully
grown and wearing an armor and helmet, from Zeus'
head—hence her association with both wisdom and
strength.

Zeus' relationship with his long-suffering wife, Hera,
gave rise to many mythological stories. For one
example, when she originally refused his advances, he
tricked her: Aware of her affection for vulnerable
animals, he transformed himself into a cuckoo and

pretended to shiver outside her window in the cold. When she took pity on the bird and held it to her breast to warm it, Zeus transformed back into himself and raped her. In her shame (and, one expects, especially through her later behavior—anger), she agrees to marry Zeus, and they have four children, including Ares: Eileithyia, Hebe, and Hephaestus, the god of fire.

Hera, however, does get some measure of revenge on Zeus. She constantly works against the heroes that Zeus champions (and, you know, fathered with other women), thwarting Hercules and Perseus at every turn. She also organized a direct rebellion against Zeus with the other gods; his absolute judgment had grown weary to the others. So, Hera drugged Zeus, and the others tied him with magical rope and absconded with his famous thunderbolt. He was saved, ironically, by one of the Titans that he had freed, who had overheard the gods talking of their betrayal, and snuck in to untie Zeus. In his fury, he had Hera hanged from the heavens in golden shackles, ignoring her cries, as did the other gods who feared his wrath. He finally relented and released her—but only after she promised never to rebel against him again.

There are also numerous myths regarding Zeus and his seductions of mortal women. In one instance, the priestess Semele was impregnated by Zeus in eagle form. When she began boasting of her alliance with Zeus, Hera became enraged; she disguised herself as a nurse and goaded Semele into asking Zeus to reveal himself in his full, god-like glory, knowing what would happen. Zeus revealed himself to Semele, and her mortal being could not handle his brilliance: She burned to death at the sight of his true self. Still, her child survived, as Zeus carried him to term by sewing him into his thigh. Their offspring would be the god Dionysius.

Aside from Semele, there is the famous tale of Leda and the Swan. The beautiful daughter of the King Aetolia and wife of the King of Sparta, Leda attracted the attention of the lustful Zeus; he disguised himself as a swan, flew down from Olympus, and in the guise of protecting her from a fierce eagle, mated with and impregnated her. Their daughter, Helen of Troy, became the most beautiful woman in the ancient world, possessing the "face that launched a thousand ships"—referring to her kidnapping by Paris of Troy and the subsequent war that followed.

Zeus also pursued the lovely Europa, who was considered the epitome of femininity at the time. He turned himself into a stunning white bull and mixed within her father's herds. She thought the bull quite beautiful and began stroking its flanks, eventually climbing onto its back. Zeus took the opportunity to gallop away with her, kidnapping her to the island of Crete, and consummating his desire. This particular story has been represented visually many times in art history—Europa is the antecedent to the name for the continent of Europe.

Ganymede was another subject of Zeus' affections, and perhaps fared better than most. When Zeus ultimately decided to abduct her, he took her to Mount Olympus to be with him among the gods. In a rare sense of obligation, Zeus decided to compensate her father, the King of Troy, with immortal horses. Ganymede stayed on Olympus, serving as cup-bearer to the gods, and was granted immortal youth. She is both the inspiration behind the constellation Aquarius (and later, zodiac sign) and the name of one of Uranus' moons.

While many of the myths featuring Zeus are about his many seductions, he also interacted with—and passed judgment on—men, both mortal and not. For one example, Zeus had a contentious relationship with the Titan, Prometheus. It began with Zeus' initial displeasure with humankind: They had offered him only bones instead of meat, at one point, so he took away the gift of fire. Prometheus defied Zeus and returned fire to the humans, thus paving the way for the progress of human civilization. Zeus was enraged by the disobedience and had Prometheus chained to a rock, with his representative animal, the eagle, pecking away at his liver each day. While Zeus was generally considered a friend of humanity, he did not truck with disobedience, and Prometheus was the one to pay the price.

Ultimately, humankind itself had to suffer the wrath of Zeus. In a story familiar to anyone who attended Bible school, Zeus became displeased with the depravity and disrespect of humankind. So, with the assistance of his brother, the sea god, Poseidon, he flooded the Earth with the aim to destroy all humankind. However, two people survived—Deucalion and his wife, Pyrrha. They made offerings to Zeus to placate him and asked how they could go about repopulating the earth. He said to throw their mother's bones over their shoulders, so the threw rocks (from Gaia, Mother Earth) into the sea, which turned into men and women.

Regardless of these rare moments of wrath, Zeus ultimately enjoyed a reputation as a fair judge, and negotiated peace between the gods and rival factions of humans, as well. There are remains of great temples to Zeus all over Greece, the most famous being the temple at Olympia, where the ancient Olympic Games were held. It was here where one of the wonders of the ancient world stood: An enormous gold and ivory statue of Zeus said to be the largest in existence at the time. Zeus was the father, not only of the Olympians and the heroes, but also the protector of all humankind. He was allied to no city-state in particular, as he was the patron of all.

CHAPTER 4:
Epic Prominence: Poseidon and Athena

Besides Zeus, and, to a lesser degree, his wife Hera, the most prominent gods in the Greek pantheon are Poseidon, the god of the sea, and Athena, the goddess of wisdom. Poseidon, as the brother of Zeus, and the reigning deity over all of the seas and its tributaries, is often regarded as the most ferocious of the gods; certainly, Poseidon is a prominent disrupter of human plans, and figures significantly in *The Odyssey*. Athena, the favorite daughter of Zeus, is both a champion of wisdom and a strong warrior. She and Poseidon are sometimes at odds, as Odysseus is Athena's prized hero.

Aside from being instrumental in the Olympians defeat of the Titans, Poseidon is perhaps the most powerful god following Zeus. While Zeus rules the skies and the heavens, Poseidon rules the vast sea—a sacred and crucial space for a seafaring people—and all the many waterways in the world. He is depicted most often with his mighty trident and long, flowing beard and hair; his eyes always look fierce, and his countenance is typically somber: This is not a god to mess with.

Poseidon's wife was a Nereid, or "sea nymph", and she bore him one son, Triton. But, as with Zeus, Poseidon was a lustful fellow, and fathered many other children via mortal and immortal lovers. Most notably, Theseus, the hero of Athens, Orion, the Hunter of constellation fame, and Polyphemus, the great Cyclops that Odysseus encounters on his meandering way back home. Poseidon also fathered the winged-horse Pegasus with the snake-headed Medusa and the sea monster, Charybdis, who was responsible for wrecking many ships with her disastrous whirlpools. Thus, Poseidon's children are also a fierce and mighty lot—from heroes to monsters and hybrids—that figure in many myths of their own.

Poseidon was one of the actors in the rebellion against Zeus, led by Hera. His punishment was to build walls around the city of Troy—while stripped of his divine powers—with a fellow rebellious god, Apollo. The King of Troy promised a great reward, but then ultimately reneged on that promise. In Poseidon's vengeance, he sent a sea monster— perhaps the famed Kraken—to attack the city. This monster was allegedly later slain by the hero Heracles (or Hercules).

The sea god also played an outsized role in the life of the epic hero, Odysseus. First, Poseidon actually participates in the Trojan War where Odysseus is off fighting; in *The Iliad* (wherein Odysseus is a secondary character), Poseidon often disguises himself as one of the Greek soldiers, giving rousing speeches and even leading them into battle on occasion. Yet, as with many gods, Poseidon is not above switching allegiances—it's indeed sometimes helpful for the plot—and did, in fact, help the Trojan, Aeneas, escape from the Greek hero, Achilles. Thus, Poseidon is not necessarily on any one side, but what suits his own whims—or desires for revenge. In *The Odyssey*, Poseidon essentially undergirds the entire plot: Because Odysseus blinded Poseidon's Cyclops son, Polyphemus (to be fair, Polyphemus was going to eat Odysseus and his men), Poseidon condemned Odysseus to wander the sea for ten years. This drives the saga of *The Odyssey* in almost its entirety: Odysseus wanders the sea, yearning for home, while his faithful wife, Penelope, waits for him. Of course, many adventures ensue along the way—that's what makes it an epic. Read Chapter 8 for more on *The Odyssey*.

Poseidon also plays a role in the establishment of the great city-state of Athens. He and Athena are vying for the chance to be the patron god of this great city, so they both offer a gift to the Athenians who will then choose which gift is more useful. Poseidon strikes his trident upon the ground, creating a spring to well up; however, the water was a bit too salty for the inhabitants' tastes. Athena, on the other hand, offers them an olive tree, so the Athenians choose her as their patron goddess. This, then, establishes a long-standing rivalry between Poseidon and Athena, who, in addition to besting Poseidon in the Athens contest, sponsors Odysseus as her favorite.

Athena, for her part, appears to be one of the most—if not *the* most—revered gods in the Greek pantheon. This could be because she appears so often in the two great epics that define ancient Greece for the modern audience—*The Iliad* and *The Odyssey*—as well as other foundational myths. But it is undoubtedly true that the "grey-eyed goddess," known for her wisdom and strength, is everywhere in the most important places in ancient Greek mythology.

Born out of the head of her father, Zeus (see the previous chapter), Athena is almost always depicted with her helmet and spear, eternally ready for battle. She is the champion of heroes, most notably Odysseus, who shares many traits with her; Odysseus is frequently cited (and either bemoaned or praised) for his wily ways, and his trickster intelligence which both gets him into and out of trouble. Both Athena and Odysseus are inveterate liars, employing the skill with abandon in order to get what they need; this is not seen, most often, as an immoral or unethical thing to do. It is simply an artful skill that is needed in dangerous times. In fact, Odysseus is often described as having grey eyes, just like his patron goddess.

But Athena sponsored other heroes, too, such as Jason of the Argonauts, and Perseus, the hero of Mycenae. It is Athena who gives Perseus the highly polished shield that will help him defeat the Gorgon, Medusa—it was also Athena who created Medusa— in punishment for her defilement of one of Athena's temples (Medusa was raped within the temple: It seems hardly fair that she herself should be punished, but this was a world before psychological acuity and/or female rights). She also sponsors the great Heracles (better known to us as Hercules, the Roman iteration of his name), helping him through many of his infamous twelve labors.

As patron god of Athens, Athena represented peace and stability—much like the beloved olive tree that she gifted her citizens. She was the adoptive mother of the first king of Athens, and, unlike many of the other gods, Athena was notably virtuous; one of her epithets is Athena Parthenos, or Athena the Virgin. The 5th century BCE temple in Athens, the famed Parthenon, was in fact built in honor of Athena. Thus, she lives on in one of the most recognizable symbols of Greece itself.

The rivalry between the ferocious Poseidon and the equally-fierce Athena can also be viewed as a parable:

They represented warring factions of city-states or internecine battles for control. They are also indicative of male versus female power—and, for that, we must be grateful that the Greeks gave us such worthy, equally-matched opponents.

CHAPTER 5:
All's fair in Love and War: Aphrodite and Ares

The beautiful Aphrodite and her constant companion, Ares—a lover, father of many of her children, and her brother—are the subject of many fascinating myths, especially the notoriously-seductive Aphrodite. As Zeus' children, and members of the twelve Olympians, the goddess of love and the god of war were, quite literally, made for each other. Her feminine aspects of divine beauty and sexual attraction were said to be the only things that could keep Ares, infamous for his temper and aggressive behavior, in check.

The legend of Aphrodite's birth is a contradictory one—one that has inspired artists throughout the century. In one version, she is created out of sea foam, fully grown—a product of the seed of Cronus after his defeat by Zeus. In other versions, she is the daughter of Zeus and one of the Titans. Even the greatest Greek authors, such as Homer and Plato, weighed in on which version was closer to the truth. The first version is favored, as it shows Aphrodite at her most beautiful and spontaneous expression, while it also allies her more closely to the Olympians. The first version of the myth also allies her more closely to the sea and to the bright star of Venus (her Romanized name) who guided sailors in the night.

Aphrodite, beautiful as she was, could be troublesome because of that very beauty, and her own lusty ways. Thus, Hera had her wed to the crippled god of fire, Hephaestus, to whom she was less than faithful, of course. Among her offspring are Eros (Love) and the great, but tragic Trojan hero, Aeneas. While she sowed some discord with her multiple affairs, she was seen as the goddess of harmony—a consensus builder who could bring disparate peoples together. As such, she was the patron goddess of city leaders.

One of her more famous affairs was with the mortal, Adonis—also the subject of numerous depictions in visual art throughout the centuries. The young lad was so stunningly attractive that Aphrodite kept him locked in a chest so only she could have him. She enlisted the help of Persephone, the reluctant wife of Hades, to guard him, only to find that Persephone had fallen in love with him, too. In the end, Zeus himself had to intervene, and directed that the women share him, each getting four months out of the year with him. Unfortunately, he was killed while hunting, and Aphrodite transformed him into a flower, as lovely as he was.

More infamous, still, was Aphrodite's relationship to Ares, her brother, and diametric opposite. They were frequent and shameless lovers, and Ares was the father to Eros and several other children of Aphrodite's. It was tacitly tolerated by the gods, for the most part, because Aphrodite calmed the notoriously aggressive Ares in the moments they were together. Still, her husband didn't much care for the arrangement, and in one mythical tale, he constructed a magical golden bed that, when the couple reached the heights of their passion, entrapped them with chains. He then had Helios, the sun god, shine his light upon their shame for all the gods to see. Once freed, they fled to different sanctuaries—but only for a time, as their love story, while perhaps shocking to our contemporary eyes, was certainly one of the most remarkable in mythological history.

Aphrodite was also instrumental in the Trojan War, in particular, with regard to the Judgment of Paris. At the wedding of Peleus and Thetis, who would beget the nearly-invincible hero, Achilles, one of the lesser goddesses offered a golden apple to whoever was judged the most beautiful goddess, out of Hera, Athena, and Aphrodite. Zeus appointed Paris of Troy to be the judge. Each of the goddesses offered something valuable to Paris to sway his decision: Athena offered him strength; Hera offered him land, but Aphrodite offered him the most beautiful mortal woman in the world. Paris chose Aphrodite, and the goddess made good on her promise, delivering Helen to Troy, thus igniting the Trojan War. Helen was already wed to the Greek king, Menelaus, so the Greek armies amassed to retrieve her and restore their honor. There were, of course, other territorial conflicts that contributed, but the most famous story remains the story of Helen of Troy.

Ares, for his part, was active in the Trojan War—as the god of war, he relished the conflict. In addition, he sided with the Trojans rather than the Greeks, perhaps in defense of Aphrodite. This does not endear him to Athena, in particular, as well as the other gods who were supportive of the Greeks. *The Iliad* shows Ares in a very unflattering light, as a ruthless and immoral killer, who is soundly bested by the wiles and strength of Athena. He is wounded on the battlefield, and complains to Zeus of his ill-treatment by Athena; the complaints fall on deaf ears, though Ares is healed.

He is always depicted in full battle gear, with a helmet, shield, and sword, and his relationships with the other gods were contentious at best—except, as stated above, his relationship with Aphrodite. The exception to the general disdain for Ares was Sparta. This military city-state considered Ares its patron, and there were tributes to him throughout the ancient city.

Perhaps his most famous encounter was in his battle with Heracles (Hercules, as we are more commonly have known him). One of Ares' sons was causing trouble, robbing and harassing pilgrims on their way to the Oracle of Delphi. Zeus sent Heracles to dispatch the unruly son, and Ares was understandably furious—even though his son had been acting reprehensibly. So, Ares challenged Heracles to a battle, thinking that he, as the god of war, would easily best the demi-god. However, Athena protected Heracles, who even managed to wound Ares, puncturing his pride.

Aphrodite is central to so many famous myths of Greek culture, while Ares exists mainly as a foil to others. In Roman times, once the Greek pantheon is adopted, Ares becomes Mars and takes on a new role as a great general and military protector. Again, each society creates the god that best suits their needs at the time.

CHAPTER 6:
Gods of Everyday Life: Food, Wine, Beauty

Aside from the gods and goddesses mentioned above, these last six complete the council of twelve: Demeter, Artemis, Hephaestus, Dionysius, Apollo, and Hermes. Demeter oversees the harvest and fertility, while Artemis the huntress retrieves heartier sustenance. Dionysius presides over the wine barrels and attendant wild revelry, and Apollo provides the music and poetry in all his resplendent beauty. Hermes functions to relay the gods' messages to us mortals, and bridges the gap between Earth and Mount Olympus. These are the patron gods and goddesses of the elements we need in order to make and celebrate a good, prosperous life.

Demeter is the goddess of fertility and harvest, and as such, is one of the oldest gods in the Greek pantheon, almost certainly predating the final sorting of the

Twelve Olympians. Fertility goddesses were worshipped throughout the ancient world, dating back to the beginning of archeological records. The most famous tale in Greek mythology regarding Demeter is that of her difficult relationship with her daughter, Persephone. Hades, the god of the underworld, kidnapped Persephone and took her prisoner with him. In Demeter's grief and anger, she caused a drought that lasted for many seasons. Finally, Zeus gave in, and forced Hades to release Persephone. However, Hades wasn't letting his prize go so easily: He placed a pomegranate seed on her tongue before her return to earth, which in some versions of the myth, meant she would long to return to him, due to the juicy sweetness (also symbolic of sexuality). In other versions, it is said that, to eat of any food of the underworld is to imprison them there forever. In the end, Zeus created a compromise wherein Persephone would spend half the year on Earth with her mother, Demeter, and the other half in the underworld with Hades. The story likely symbolizes the seasons, with Persephone's release to Earth as the coming of spring each year, and her return to the underworld as the end of the harvest.

Artemis, the goddess of the hunt, is a changeable and complex figure. In some stories, she is regarded as another goddess of fertility, and by her association with the waxing and waning of the moon, of childbirth. In other stories, however, she is notably fierce and undeniably dangerous. She had asked Zeus to allow her not to marry, so she could remain chaste and dedicate herself to hunting and the outdoors. Thus, she does not take kindly to those who wish to violate her—as in our modern sensibilities, seems quite right. She infamously killed the great hunter, Orion, after he attempted to rape her and/or one of her colleagues. She also kills the daughters of Niobe after the woman boasted that she had the greatest powers of childbirth overall. She slays the hunter Aktaion for boasting that he was the better hunter. And she dispatched a wild boar to destroy the city of

Kalydon after its offerings were insufficient. Artemis was the embodiment of the wilder aspects of the feminine spirit, and she was both celebrated and feared for her ferocity.

Hephaestus was the god of fire, born crippled or deformed, depending on the telling. In fact, his father Zeus threw him from the heavens after his birth, so hideous was he. Nevertheless, he turns out to be a brilliant engineer and craftsman, and is usually depicted with his blacksmith's tools. He is said to have not only created the great Labyrinth for King Minos to ensnare the Minotaur, but also to have literally created the first woman, Pandora, out of clay. He was married off to Aphrodite, who, as we learned in the previous chapter, was not the most faithful of wives.

Dionysius is the raucous god of wine and revelry, wherein we get the adverb "Dionysian" to describe a party of epic proportions. He is also associated with ecstasy and madness, the kind of psychological unrestrained "id" to the more civilized powers in the pantheon. He is often surrounded by satyrs and fauns—half-man, half-goat creatures—thus emphasizing his animalistic nature underneath his anthropomorphic exterior. In some stories, it is suggested that he is the only god who is actually half mortal—the son of the phoenician Semele and the god Zeus. This again serves to showcase his in-between status, not neatly fitting into one world or the other.

Apollo was the glowing representation of youth and beauty, and he was one of the most favored gods because of this. He is the patron god of the arts, music, and poetry; he symbolizes the best that civilization has to offer. However, as with all of the gods, he could be a changeable deity, and he was also instrumental (as with Artemis) in the slaying of Niobe's children, as well as playing a hand in the death of Achilles. Nevertheless, most often, Apollo is thought of as a kind of sun god, radiant in his youth and beauty.

Hermes is the messenger of the gods, relaying messages from Olympus down to the mortals below. He was also the patron god of merchants and—perhaps ironically—thieves: Basically, Hermes oversaw the basic everyday rules of commerce and financial prosperity. He was also something of a trickster, stealing Poseidon's trident, Artemis' arrows, and Aphrodite's girdle; perhaps this mayhem represented the inherent stability in the markets he was supposed to oversee. Hermes is also instrumental in *The Odyssey*, helping Odysseus find his way home.

While Zeus and the other major gods are disrupting the heavens and the earth with their powers and battles, these everyday gods oversee the basic elements of daily life for humans. They, too, are surrounded by adventurous tales and fantastical myths, yet they also fulfill a need for the humans that worship them—that of security and comfort: Food and wine, revelry and art, and a connection to the gods themselves.

PART II: Culture and Legends

Greek culture and mythology weave a tight web of mores, passing down information about how people act, and should act, and why the world works the way it does. This is what legends, myths, and morality tales are for: To indicate to the listener (or, these days, reader) how good people behave, how bad people are punished, and thus, what values we should uphold. They are our links to the glorious and ancient past, telling us *who they were* and *what they believed.* They are also explanatory, describing how the weather works, for example, in a time before meteorology; it is no coincidence that, in all mythological traditions, there is the inevitable god of thunder (Zeus; Lugh in the Celtic; Thor in the Norse) and many gods of the harvest and of fertility (Demeter and Aphrodite). These stories speculate about why certain things happen by assigning powers to gods and other supernatural beings: This was a way of making sense of a chaotic world, and understanding our place in it.

It was also a method of protection: If you pray to a certain god or goddess, or if you practice a certain ritual, or if you observe appropriate customs, then you will avoid suffering and enjoy prosperity. This also serves as a way to assign responsibility elsewhere for events that happen outside of your control ("It was too wet this year for a good harvest; our offerings to Demeter weren't enough"). Concomitantly, it was a cause for celebration and feasting when events are auspicious.

Greek culture and its legendary stories share many similarities with other mythological canons: Magic is all around, utilized to explain the inexplicable; heroes boast superhuman strength, sometimes divine origins, and make good use of hard-won wisdom; gods can be trickster figures or helpers, depending on the context; adventures abound; romance is complicated and sometimes tragic; battles are forever being waged, and warriors are forever being supplanted. There is always the constant reminder of the fragility of life, in the fear over land and harvest, the brutality and bounty of the sea. Loyalty and bravery and sacrifice are tantamount; heroic deeds cement one's place in history, and as it turns out, there truly is no place like home. Philosophical ideas and divine order merge to create a culture of splendid ideas, and the tales that are told here have reverberated throughout the Western world for centuries upon centuries.

CHAPTER 7:
Kleos: The Iliad and the Glory of War

The two greatest epic poems in the whole of Western literature are, almost without a doubt: *The Iliad* and *The Odyssey*. Deriving from the much older oral tradition, these two poems were written down and formalized by the blind poet, Homer, during the Classical age of Greece, at the height of its literary and artistic achievements. In the next chapter, you will learn more about Odysseus and his exploits. Here, we will look at an overview of *The Iliad*—the great epic detailing one of the longest, fiercest, and most contentious battles in Western history.

Epic poems are a special brand of literary achievement that sets them apart from the regular poem. Epic poems must be long, narrative poems that typically set out to glorify a particular hero and his (or her, though rarely) role in the fate of a people or a nation. Both poems follow the five basic epic conventions, as originally set out by Homer: A semi-divine hero with supernatural qualities, the ideal representative of a culture; a vast setting, geographically speaking, often including the underworld; courageous action; the intervention of the gods; an expansive style of writing, even ceremonial at times. There are other epic conventions, but these are the five that define the epic poem. Usually, the epic begins *en medias res*—in the middle of things—which heightens the sense of urgency and drama; there are also long catalogs of people or items, and repetition of stock phrases used to describe key characters or events. As the epic poem came out of the oral tradition, these last two made the poems easier to memorize and recite.

In *The Iliad*, our hero is Achilles. The reader is dropped into the final year of the decade-long Trojan War. The Greeks (or Achaeans) have been trying to lay siege to the great city of Troy after Paris has kidnapped Helen from King Menelaus (with the assistance of Aphrodite). At the beginning of *The Iliad*, Achilles is brooding and refuses to fight: Agamemnon, brother to Menelaus and a great warrior in his own right, has stolen away Achilles' desire, the lovely Briseis. His intransigence and pride nearly cost the Greeks the war, and the poem itself is more concerned with the idea of fate: Everyone is subject to the vagaries of fate—even the blessed and heroic.

Agamemnon decides to storm the city walls without Achilles but is quite unsuccessful, making him unpopular with the soldiers. Paris, the god-like hero of Troy, challenges Menelaus to a one-on-one battle to determine the end of the war straight away. They fight, Paris decked out in ridiculously beautiful armor—he is being teased as something of a dandy—and Menelaus is clearly the superior warrior. However, the gods intercede, in the form of Aphrodite, who whisks Paris away, safely ensconced in a cloud. The war was not to be settled so easily.

While there are still twenty books of the epic poem to go, the action suddenly shifts to Olympus and the gods, who are arguing over the fate of Troy. Hera and Athena wish to see it destroyed, both being wronged by Paris prior to the war (he choose Aphrodite as the most beautiful), but Zeus does not. Eventually, after much haranguing, Zeus relents and acquiesces that Troy will fall—though he will have his revenge at some point, destroying other cities in exchange. The gods are not always kind, and, just like the humans they oversee, can be petty.

The action returns to the battlefield, where the great warrior Diomedes lays waste to many men, even attacking Ares and Aphrodite. Only with Apollo's intervention, is his ferocious attack repelled. Diomedes continues his raging, squaring off against the Trojan, Glaucus—but, curiously, instead of fighting, the two begin to talk and realize that they have similar backgrounds. In addition, there is a scene showing the Trojan hero, Hector's wife,

Andromache, worried for her husband. The poet's point in including scenes like these is to emphasize that there is always the question of humanity in war; there are always actual people with actual lives who are impacted by the bloodshed of wartime.

Hector then takes center stage, challenging any Greek to hand-to-hand combat. Ajax is recruited, and they clash without a decisive—that is, death—blow, though Ajax proves himself the better fighter. Darkness falls, and they must disengage. The next day, there is a momentary truce, while the dead are cleared away. Again, the emphasis here on humanity in battle is notable.

Hector then leads a charge against the entire Greek army, and Zeus has forbidden the gods to intervene: Hector successfully drives the Greek soldiers back behind their encampment, and it appears that the Trojans might be headed for victory. Indeed, Menelaus sends Odysseus and some other men to persuade Achilles to rejoin the fighting; he still yet refuses, which will cost the Greeks many lives, as well as very nearly the war.

Hector and his men continue successfully beating back the Greeks, eventually smashing through their camp walls. The Greeks begin fleeing to their ships, and it looks as if all will be lost. However, none other than Poseidon himself intervenes, rallying the Greeks and spurring them on to drive the Trojans back. At the same time, Hera distracts Zeus from this turn of events by seducing him. Although Zeus has already agreed to allow Troy to fall, the gods can so often be changeable, so Hera keeps him occupied—for a time.

When Zeus awakens and realises what has happened, he calls Poseidon to stand down, and, again, Hector and the Trojans gain an advantage. Hector calls for his men to burn the Greek ships, effectively cutting off their means of escape.

In their most desperate hour, a new kind of hero emerges in the figure of Patroclus: He is the best friend of Achilles, and the only one capable of persuading Achilles to re-enter the war. He pleads with Achilles, who eventually relents, and with the help of the Myrmidons—the soldiers loyal to Achilles—they are able to stop the ships from burning. Patroclus, in his excitement at their success and his foolhardy bravery, decides to start charging towards the Trojans, driving them back to the city. Apollo intervenes, striking Patroclus' armor off his body so that Hector can cleanly pierce him with a spear. Now, Achilles' wrath will not be contained, and the fate of the city is most definitely sealed. There is an interlude to retrieve the body and mourn the loss of Patroclus, wherein Achilles gives a lengthy speech on the goodness of his fallen friend. He also reconciles with Menelaus, and they resolve to carry out the battle until victorious. Achilles himself already knows that it has been prophesied that he will die in this battle—but with the death of Patroclus, he no longer cares, and he will avenge his friend whatever the outcome.

The next few books are achingly brutal, as Achilles full wrath is unleashed on the battlefield. As well, the gods have taken sides, and they are openly fighting against one another and with either the Trojans or the Greeks. The Trojans are eventually overcome and flee back behind the walls of their city—all, that is, except for Hector.

As Achilles approaches Hector, he loses his nerve; Achilles is fast and furious, indeed. He runs around the city several times before Achilles catches up with him and kills him with his spear. Not only does he kill him, but he also ties his dead body to the front of his chariot—an ignominious image of defeat, and a clear insult to Troy.

In the penultimate book, there are funeral tributes to celebrate Patroclus, with games and revelry—a welcome respite from the bloody battle scenes. The Greeks know that they will be victorious, and Achilles has slaked his thirst for revenge. In the final book, King Priam of Troy appeals to Achilles to hand over Hector's body, imploring Achilles in a moving speech to release the body. Achilles relents, hands over the body, and the poem ends.

It may seem odd that the poem begins after nearly a decade of war, and ends before that war is over and Achilles has met his fated death, but this is part of the remnants of the oral tradition. The Trojan horse filled with Greeks will enter the city, and Troy will inevitably fall. The listeners would already know the history of what came before and what will come after; they are there to be entertained by the stylized storytelling and the extreme exploits of battle and triumph. We too seek glory—*kleos*, in Greek—and gain it vicariously through the story of the great hero Achilles, and the unmatched battle for the city of Troy.

CHAPTER 8:
Nostos: The Odyssey and the Search for Home

In the previous chapter, we explored the great battles of the Trojan War, and its hero, Achilles. Here, we will look at an overview of *The Odyssey*: The great epic detailing one of the longest, most fantastic, and most magical journeys home in Western history.

Epic poems are a special brand of literary achievement that sets them apart from a regular poem. Epic poems must be long, narrative poems that typically set out to glorify a particular hero and his (or her, though rarely) role in the fate of a people or a nation. Both poems follow the five basic epic conventions, as originally set out by Homer: A semi-divine hero with supernatural qualities, the ideal representative of a culture; a vast setting, geographically speaking, often including the underworld; courageous action; the intervention of the gods; an expansive style of writing, even ceremonial at times. There are other epic conventions, but these are the five that define the epic poem. Usually, the epic begins *en medias res*—in the middle of things—which heightens the sense of urgency and drama; there are also long catalogs of people or items, and repetition of stock phrases throughout, used to describe key characters or events. As the epic poem came out of the oral tradition, these last two made the poems easier to memorize and recite.

Many scholars, and ordinary readers alike, consider *The Odyssey* to be one of the finest—if not *the* finest—work in all of Western literature. It has something for everything, from battles, to seductions, to fantastic journeys, not to mention a host of fabulous creatures, unparalleled adventures, and the intermittent intervention of the gods. No summary can truly capture its wide-ranging wonder: It is a read for anyone who has a vibrant imagination and a curious mind.

Odysseus is one of the heroes of the Trojan War, though he is barely present in *The Iliad*; he is on his way home to Ithaca (one of the Greek islands) after ten wearying years of battle, but this journey, too, will take him another decade. We know this, as Odysseus has angered Poseidon—we learn later in the book why this is—and Poseidon has sentenced him to this long, arduous journey. All the other heroes of the war have already returned safely. This journey will be one that the Greeks, as a seafaring people daily risking their lives on the open oceans, will particularly relish.

We begin as Odysseus has washed up on an island and is being held captive by the sea nymph, Calypso—one of many in a cast of sea characters in Poseidon's league. Back in Ithaca, we meet Odysseus' thus far faithful wife, Penelope, who is mobbed by many suitors—108, to be exact—vying for their chance at a kingship and Penelope's bed. We also meet Telemachus, son of Odysseus and Penelope, who is a rational young man frustrated by the situation at court. The goddess Athena urges him to amass a crew and sail out to find his father.

Telemachus sets out on a journey of his own and comes to meet the old hero, Nestor, at his kingdom in Pylos. There, Nestor tells him a truncated version of the Trojan War—this would be a device in the oral tradition to remind listeners as to what took place before—and says that the fleet was separated and he does not know what happened to Odysseus. He also relates the cautionary tale of how Agamemnon, another hero of the Trojan War, returned home, only to be killed by a usurper at home. The message to Telemachus is clear: If he leaves Ithaca in the hands of the unruly suitors for too long, the kingdom will slip away.

Telemachus gets more answers from the next Greek he meets, Menelaus, whose wife Helen's kidnapping initiated the war. He says that he was told by an old sailor that Odysseus was in the clutches of Calypso; now, Telemachus has a lead. Meanwhile, the suitors are back in Ithaca raiding Odysseus' stores, drinking his wine and eating his food: They are shown as disrespectful and loutish, disregarding one of the sacred rules of the ancient world—hospitality.

Finally, Zeus orders Calypso to free Odysseus, and even though she offers him the gift of immortality, Odysseus jumps on the chance to leave. He crafts a makeshift raft and endures twenty harrowing days in stormy seas—whipped up by Poseidon. But Athena helps her favorite hero, and he eventually washes up on the shore of Phaeacia to be taken in by the princess Nausicaa.

Nausicaa and her father, the king, agree to assist Odysseus in his journey home. But before he leaves, there must be feasting, revelry, and singing—and, of course, the most important thing: The telling of stories.

King Alcinous implores Odysseus to tell of some of his adventures, and here is where we learn of how Odysseus ran afoul of Poseidon. After escaping the land of the lotus-eaters—a lovely interlude of sleepy dreaming; a sort of poppy-induced hallucinatory interlude—Odysseus and his men arrive at the lands of the Cyclops. They are generally peaceful, in that they keep to themselves, as farmers and cheesemakers, but they are also described as lacking laws and civility in general.

The men come across the cave of one of the Cyclops, Polyphemus, and the son of Poseidon. They wait for the giant to return—availing themselves of some supplies, of course—and when he returns, he is angered by the intrusion. He devours two of Odysseus' men on the spot, traps them in his cave by sealing it with a large boulder, and takes a nap. Upon waking, he eats another two men. Odysseus hatches a plan: He gets Polyphemus drunk, trying to distract him and dull his senses. In a moment of brilliance, Odysseus tells the monster that his name is Nobody. He is then able to capitalize on the giant's drunkenness and poke out his eye—the Cyclops has only one—with a sharpened pole. The giant flings aside the boulder, roaring to the others on the island that "Nobody is trying to kill me!" So, of course, nobody comes to his aid. The men escape by tying themselves to the bellies of Polyphemus' oversized sheep and sail away. The Cyclops wails for revenge, and Poseidon gives him some comfort by delaying Odysseus' return home: Odysseus is too much a favorite of the gods to be outrightly killed.

Then, Odysseus relates the tale of how, following that adventure, he and his men are caught by the sorcerer Circe. She offers the men wine to drink, which erases their memories and turns them into pigs. Odysseus is not in the arrival party, so he escapes their fate and gets assistance from Hermes, who gives him a drug, making him immune to her potion. In exchange for returning his men to normal, the party agrees to stay with Circe for a year, the men eating and drinking their fill, and Odysseus enjoying the company and comforts of Circe herself. It is almost a love story, and ultimately, the reader is left feeling sorrier for Circe than angry.

Before Circe allows Odysseus to leave, she insists that he visit the underworld—another epic convention—to ask for directions home. The blind (and dead) prophet, Tiresias—some suggest he is a stand-in for Homer himself—tells Odysseus that he will reach home, rescue his kingdom and Penelope, and live to a ripe old age. But only if he refuses the temptation to steal the cattle of Helios, the sun god. Forewarned, Odysseus knows what he must do.

He sets off from Circe's isle, but then, more peril he must face. She warns him of the Sirens—deadly half-human creatures whose voices will at first sound pleasant, but will eventually drive men to madness and make them plunge to their death. So, Odysseus has his men plug their ears with wax, and he himself—curious to hear the Sirens fatal call—has himself lashed to the mast. Surviving this, Odysseus is also forewarned about the nine-headed sea monster, Scylla, and the deadly whirlpool, Charybdis, managing to escape them, barely. However, as the men sail on, they get stuck on Helios' island, where storms keep them stuck there for many days. Some of the men get so desperately hungry that they slaughter some of the cattle while Odysseus is sleeping. Retribution is swift, and once they set sail, their ship is broken apart, but Odysseus is spared, finally washing up ashore on Calypso's island.

The storytelling over, King Alcinous and Princess Nausicaa bade Odysseus farewell and helped him set

sail. He shortly lands in Ithaca, though his adventure
is not quite over. It has been ten years of war in
Troy, and a further ten years journey to get home, but
Odysseus must now reclaim his kingdom and his
queen.

There is an interlude during which Odysseus travels
through his land, marveling at being home, but
unaware of how he will be received. A kind
swineherd, Eumaeus, an old servant of Odysseus,
takes him and gives him food and wine. Odysseus
claims to be an old Cretan warrior—a hallmark of
Odysseus, that he disguises himself frequently—and
listens to Eumaeus tell of what a lovely man
Telemachus has turned out to be.

Meanwhile, Athena has told Telemachus to return to
Ithaca, as his father has returned and there will be
trouble with the suitors. Telemachus arrives at the
hut of Eumaeus, and Odysseus reveals his true self;
they embrace with unbridled emotion. Odysseus then

tells Telemachus to return to the palace and remove all the weapons from the great hall. Odysseus will return shortly thereafter, disguised as a beggar.

Odysseus shows up in Court, dismayed by the disrespect of the suitors and the state of his kingdom. He sees Penelope—made even more beautiful than in her natural middle age by Athena—while she persuades the suitors all to give her a lavish gift. Odysseus is not certain what to think, but he speaks with her in his disguise, praising her for staying loyal to her husband, and she reveals to him how she had fought hard to keep all the suitors away. He is convinced by her loyalty, and the final plan is hatched. Penelope tells Odysseus that she will hold a shooting competition to determine who the best of the suitors is.

The following day, Penelope retrieves Odysseus' old bow and tells the suitors to fire an arrow through twelve ax-heads to win her hand. The bow is so mighty that not one of the suitors can even string it, much less shoot an arrow. Odysseus, still in disguise, has the doors to the great hall blocked, then strides up, takes the bow and fires twelve arrows directly into twelve ax-heads. Zeus sends down a peal of thunder, and Odysseus throws off his beggar's cloak to reveal his true identity.

He mercilessly slaughters the suitors, one by one, with his bow and arrows. The scene is one of horrific carnage in a relatively bloodless tale, but Odysseus must prove that he is the greatest hero and the rightful king. It is over in one lopsided battle.

Finally, Odysseus and Penelope are reunited—a tender scene wherein they recount what had happened to them in the twenty years they've been separated. Their marriage bed is carved of an olive tree—symbolic of peace and strength of unity—and Odysseus' knowledge of that proves to Penelope that he is, indeed, her long-overdue husband. After a short battle with the families of the dead suitors, Odysseus is victorious, and peace is reestablished in Ithaca.

As Achilles proved his quest of glory, so did Odysseus prove his desire for *nostos*—the Greek word for "home". While war and battle are all well and good, at the end of the day, a man wants more than to prove himself—he wants home and hearth, and the love of family. In this way, these epics tell the essential tale of what it means to be human—not only in ancient Greece, but throughout our shared history.

CHAPTER 9:
Jason and the Argonauts: Another Epic Journey

Another rollicking tale, though not set in epic fashion, is the story of Jason and his Argonauts. His search for the legendary Golden Fleece, while perhaps not as epic as Odysseus' journey, is still one for the ages. His wife, Medea, is also a prominent figure in Greek literary history for her role in Euripides' great dramatic tragedy, *Medea*. The exploits of Jason and his men were told throughout and beyond the Greek isles for centuries.

Having been stripped of his kingdom in Iolkos by his uncle, Jason was sent away to the forests of Mount Pelion. There, he was educated by the famous centaur, Cheiron (centaurs were famed for their wisdom; hence, JK Rowling's use of Firenze as a teacher in the Harry Potter series). As he came of age, Jason gained a reputation of being a strong warrior and a good hunter; he participated in the famous hunt for the Calydonian boar, who terrorized the region.

He finally returned to take his rightful place in the kingdom of Iolkos. On the journey, he lost one of his sandals, which prompted Pelias—the usurper—to recall a long-ago prophecy: That he would be killed by the man with one sandal. In his fear, Pelias decided to send Jason away on a quest for the fabled Golden Fleece—a journey thought to be impossible, and, most likely, fatal. Jason, like young men during this age of adventure, gladly took up the task. He would not only capture the Golden Fleece, but also gain both glory and a kingdom in the bargain.

The legend of the Golden Fleece suggests that it was sheared from a golden ram owned by the messenger god, Hermes. The ram was sent by a minor goddess to save her children from the attacking Thebians; only the son survived, but he promptly made a sacrifice to

the gods for sending this magical ram to save him.
He placed its Golden Fleece in a sacred grove of Ares
on Colchis, where it was guarded by a fearsome
serpent. The allure of the Golden Fleece was that it
could provide the ultimate protection for anyone who
wore it.

Jason, like Odysseus, is another favorite of Athena's,
and she helps him to build a magnificent ship, the
Argo, and amass a steady crew—the Argonauts. The
ship itself contained a magical plank of wood, from
Zeus, with the power of speech, and could hold more
than fifty men. The Argonauts were a very worthy
cast of Greek heroes, including Hercules, Peleus, and
Orpheus, among others.

On the voyage to Colchis, our hero and his men
encounter many fantastic creatures and peoples—
much like Odysseus did. One of their more famous
tales involves the blind Phineus. They land upon the
island of Thrace and hear of the troubles of Phineus:

He has been blinded for revealing the future to humankind. Thus, he is also tormented by great Harpies, sent down by Zeus, that would swoop down and steal his food at any chance. Two of the Argonauts—wing-footed brothers—were fated to save him from the Harpies. So, they set a trap of food, and the brothers chased the Harpies to the ends of the Earth—forbidden to kill Zeus' creatures—before returning to the ship.

Jason and his men were also—like Odysseus—nearly ensnared by the women of Lemnos; the entrapment of men by magical women is a running theme in many of the Greek mythologies. They were set upon by giants at the island of Doliones, and eventually lost Hercules when his lover was stolen by the sea nymphs, and he set off to rescue her.

When they arrive at Colchis, the king is more than reluctant to hand over the Golden Fleece, simply, so he invents a series of arduous tasks—reminiscent of the twelve labors of Hercules—for Jason to complete in order to win the Golden Fleece. First, he and his men were to plow a field with fire-breathing bulls, so they can then plant the serpent's teeth into the tilled ground. Then, they would be required to fend off the giants who would spring out of the magical serpent's teeth. Impossible tasks, indeed, but Jason has Athena on his side: She sent Eros (daughter of Aphrodite) down to make the witch Medea fall in love with Jason. Medea knows of magic spells and potions, and ends up being of great help to Jason. She brews a potion to tame the bulls and recommends that Jason start a battle among the giants themselves so they would leave the Argonauts and the kingdom at Colchis alone.

Despite completing his assigned tasks, Jason is still denied the Golden Fleece. Again, Medea is instrumental: She shows Jason the hidden location of the Fleece and gives him yet another potion to drug the guardian serpent. Jason is successful in spiriting away the Golden Fleece to his great ship, Argo, with Medea in tow.

After another eventful journey home, Jason and the Argonauts return triumphant—with still more help from the talented Medea. She even helped to rid Iolkos of the usurper, Pelias, convincing his daughters that, if they cut up their father and boiled him in her magic potion, they would gain everlasting youth. This, of course, was the end of Pelias. However, Jason himself did not take the throne, instead, settling in Corinth. He seemed to want to put his adventures behind him, as did Odysseus and Hercules at the end of their wild tales: All three heroes settled with families and tended to their lands until tragedy intervened (at least in the cases of Hercules and Jason).

He marries Medea, and they have three sons, living happily together for many years. But, alas, Jason becomes enchanted by Glauce, daughter of the king of Corinth—perhaps he was bewitched; perhaps the intervention of the gods had a hand; perhaps it was simply weak human nature. In any event, Medea murdered Glauce, and then, rather than risk losing them to capture or enslavement, she murdered her own children and fled to Athens. This last, most tragic part of the story is that which is taken up by Euripides in his play, *Medea*. Jason, for his part, lost the favor of Hera—the goddess of marriage—because of his betrayal of Medea, and died lonely and unhappy.

Combining the elements of Odysseus' fantastic journey with tales similar to the tasks of Hercules, the story of Jason and his Argonauts is yet another mythological story about the characters of heroes, the perils of the wide world, and the ultimate joy of coming home. That Jason's story ends in tragedy is a cautionary tale of what comes to those who disturb the powerful bonds and duties that is *nostos*—"home".

CHAPTER 10:
Tales of Trial and Error:
Tantalus, Sisyphus, Midas

There are other cautionary tales within ancient Greek mythology. Like the parables in the Biblical text, they are meant as a warning to us mortals about the limits of desire. These three kings were legendary for their horrific deeds and mighty greed. Each, in turn, was meted a punishment befitting of their errors.

Tantalus was a depraved king of Sipylus—a mortal born of immortal parents—one of the first generations of humans to come out of Olympus. He was fabulously wealthy and famously wicked, egregiously flouting the power and order of the gods. In the time of the first humans, the mortals were allowed to dine with the gods on Mount Olympus on occasion, and Tantalus joined in. However, he was so outrageously discourteous that Zeus was absolutely furious.

There are different versions of his misbehavior: One simply suggests that he gossiped to other mortals about the gods' plans for them—disobedient enough, one supposes, but not so dire as to invite eternal punishment. Another version says that he ate of the forbidden food of the gods—disobedient again, and reminiscent of a later story that would be told in Genesis. A final version is the most (pardon the pun) tantalizing: Tantalus decided to test the gods, to see if they really did have superior powers of knowledge. So, Tantalus had his own son chopped up and served up in a stew to the gods; only then could he be certain of their powers of discernment. Everyone recognized that something was badly amiss, of course, and Tantalus was justly and firmly punished.

Zeus quickly curses his kingdom and his dynasty, ensuring that Tantalus will leave no lasting legacy. Then, he sentences him to a particularly apt torture in the underworld: Tantalus will be positioned near a pool of water that will always shrink when he tries to drink from it. He will be under a tree where the ripest of fruits will be forever beyond his reach. Thus, Tantalus is doomed to spend eternity both thirsty and hungry—a wretched soul doomed to never-ending frustration.

Sisyphus, an early king of Corinth, gained infamy due to his general trickery and dishonesty. What seriously got him into trouble was twice cheating death. In the first instance, he managed to capture Thanatos—the personification of death—after he was killed, and had descended into Hades. With Thanatos in his grasp, no mortals could die, and it took the intervention of Ares to free Thanatos and set the natural order of things right again.

The second instance was perhaps even more audacious: Before his death, Sisyphus had convinced his wife not to provide any offerings to Hades for his trip, and to stay in the underworld. Instead, he pleads with Persephone, the reluctant wife of Hades, to take mercy on him, return him to the living where he will instruct his wife to take up the proper offerings, and then go back to the underworld. Of course, he has no intention of doing such a thing, and, therefore, angered all the gods.

Zeus was the one to mete out the punishment, and it was determined that Sisyphus in the afterlife would be doomed to an appropriate penalty. In order to discourage other mortals from attempting Sisyphus' underhanded trickery and deceit, Zeus condemned Sisyphus to the task of pushing an enormous boulder up to the top of a hill, only to have it roll back down. All his strenuous efforts would be repeated, over and over, for eternity. It does not do to mess with the natural order of things, it would appear.

Last, Midas is probably the most infamous of the three, and his tale is a familiar one to ward off unhealthy greed. The myth says that Midas comes across the famed satyr, Silenus, who was a bit worse for wear after a night of drinking and revelry. Midas gave him food and drink, and the grateful satyr granted him one wish. Midas was already a terribly wealthy king, yet he yearned for more, so he wished that everything he touched would turn to gold.

Upon returning to his kingdom, he was at first surprised and delighted that the satyr had actually granted his wish, and thus he set about turning stones into gold nuggets, and bouquets into golden flowers. The novelty of this gift quickly wore off, however, as he tried to mount his horse and it turned into a solid mass of lifeless gold. The repercussions of his wish became even more evident when he tried to eat and drink: Nothing could get past his lips without turning to gold. Of course, in some versions of the story—introduced long after the original myth—he touched his daughter, and she turned to gold, as well. In any event, Midas begged to have this ironically unfortunate gift removed, and he was directed on an arduous journey to the river Pactolus, where he could wash away his sinful desire.

Each of these myths was designed to teach a valuable lesson: Too much knowledge, too much power, and too much wealth are all too much of a good thing. Mortals have their specific place in the universe, and they should not question the gods, disobey them, or wish for more than it is their fate to have. There is value in humility—it is clear.

CHAPTER 11:
Philosophy and Divinity: A Merging of Ideas

A chapter on Greek philosophy is included here, as it is difficult to understand the ancient Greeks and their mythology—not to mention their outsized influence throughout the world—without also taking a quick look at their unique philosophy. Indeed, nearly all Western philosophy grew out of this ancient tradition in some form or another, and these points of view have generated much universal pondering. From the mystical to the logical, and from the divine to the fantastical, Greek philosophy is a fascinating syncretism of story-telling, logic, and speculation.

While there had been notable Greek philosophers prior to Socrates (Pythagoras and Democritus, for example), the tradition that is still most influential in Western culture today is that of the Socratic tradition. This tradition coincided with the Greeks' Classical period. Prior to this time, the city-states had been largely rivaling communities, sharing linguistic and cultural similarities, but vying amongst themselves for power. Athens had begun an experiment in its quest for strength: To suggest that all male citizens, no matter their wealth or power, to have equal rights within the city-state. This is what we know as "democracy". This innovative—nay, radical—idea meant that any free citizen could hold forth on whatever topic he wanted; it also meant that courts were organized, and free men could defend themselves. With this new freedom came the beginnings of philosophy, which allowed these men the intellectual space and capacity to speak in a free society. In fact, one of the most important skills taught in the early philosophical schools was rhetoric—the ability to speak and argue well.

Onto this background came Socrates, who was unlike other philosophers of the age. Instead of pondering the physical world and natural phenomena, Socrates concerned himself with virtue and the good life; he asked questions such as: "What does it mean to be a good citizen?" and "What is morality? How do we decide?" This is the beginnings of a philosophy that is separate from science or politics (though it certainly was politically controversial). In addition, Socrates did not ask for money for his teachings, as the other groups did. This was noteworthy in that, with the introduction of democracy, the old aristocracy was threatened, and the clashes between preserving their self-interests and wealth, and that of maintaining a free society became more prominent in Socrates' time. Socrates seemed firmly on the side of democratic values.

Of course, this won him powerful enemies, and, eventually, he was put on trial for spreading slanderous and harmful ideas. The court found him guilty, and he was sentenced to death—essentially, as an enemy of the state. However, this was merely a formality, as the Athenians did not actually like to impose the death penalty—it clashed with their seemingly democratic values of free speech. He was given the opportunity to flee. But Socrates would not do so, on principle, and thus he obeyed the Court, drinking a glass of poisonous hemlock. This made him an icon—more influential in his death than in his life.

The reason we know anything about Socrates is due to the writings of his student, Plato, who followed in his teacher's footsteps. Perhaps the most influential Western philosopher of all time, Plato imagined a realm of what he called "The Forms", wherein everything that we instinctively know about virtue, justice, and goodness must certainly exist. That is, in the Realm of the Forms, perfect truth exists, perfect justice exists, and perfect virtue exists—it is our job to try to recall these to the best of our ability and apply this to our imperfect world. Plato is also famous for philosophizing about the ideal city-state, which, for him would not be a democracy; instead, it would be ruled by a great philosopher-king who would know what is best and most virtuous for everyone. Yet, of course, that great philosopher-king could not really exist, for any philosopher worth his name wouldn't want that job. Thus, Plato wisely demurs about any wish he may have for power.

His student, Aristotle, continued this tradition, but with his own innovations. Aristotle suggested that, while it is wise and good to contemplate the most abstract and perfect of ideas, we must also apply these ideas using logic. He postulates that the best life is one that is lived through "virtuous action." We must thoughtfully ponder what is best, then logically act accordingly. This is a simplification, of course, but it encapsulates the core of the Aristotelian view—one that would be followed most strenuously by the Stoic philosophers of Roman times.

It is also important to note that Platonic philosophy—which is really shorthand to encompass the ideas of Socrates and Aristotle, as well as the primacy of Plato—was incorporated into much of early Christianity. The idea that the ultimate Good could be discovered in the Realm of the Forms is akin to the idea that an ultimate God could be discovered and reunited with by His followers.

Essentially, Greek philosophy challenged their citizens—and challenges us still yet today—to contemplate what kind of life we should be living, and what kind of person we should be. Socrates famously said, as recounted by Plato: "The unexamined life is not worth living." From the origins of democracy to the foundation of Western philosophy, ancient Greece is certainly worth examination.

PART III: Monsters and Heroes

There cannot be great tales if there are no great foes or great heroes: This is the very stuff that myths are made of. All myths are stories of who we'd like to be and what we'd like to have—a form of wish fulfillment. They explain the world around us and the characters that populate that world. Heroes and monsters are beacons of light and darkness, triumph and defeat, and of right-thinking and wrong-doing. We gain insight into the culture that generates these various figures, learning their values, fears and hopes.

While monsters may function in mythology to provide obstacles to heroes, it is almost always the case that the monsters also work, symbolically speaking, to hold a mirror to ourselves: What we fear and what we despise usually arise from the lesser demons of our very own natures. That is, the monsters created in mythology represent our worst fears, our secret desires, and/or our least redeeming qualities. In ancient mythology, the monster typically represents the "Other": She or he or it is a manifestation of the direct opposite of what the teller of the tale values and holds dear. Because Greco-Roman culture did not have a vision of the end of the world, as did the Egyptians and the Norse, their myths do not have one primal enemy or battle; the outlook on life was one of maintaining stability and order in the home and throughout the empire. In addition, monsters can be misread—or, certainly re-interpreted—through time: The Minotaur and Medusa can be seen as victims of circumstances beyond their control, for example. The Cyclops, Polyphemus, can be seen as a legitimate defender of his own home from the raiders—Odysseus and his men. Sympathy for monsters may be a contemporary phenomenon, but it makes us think more deeply about our own cultural biases.

Heroes follow a similar pathway in most mythologies—especially the epic poem first crafted by

Homer. He or she must undertake a journey, often perilous; on that journey, the hero must cross from the ordinary world, where the rules are understood, into an extraordinary world—the underworld, a supernatural realm, or even a foreign land—where the hero must use his or her wits to thrive. The hero faces a series of trials, sometimes with a band of allies, and must conquer his or her greatest challenge—the final test. If the hero overcomes it, then he or she will be granted some form of reward: Wealth and property; reputation and fame; security and companionship. Heroes represent the values that the society who tells his or her saga wants us to uphold, whether it be bravery in battle, or faithfulness in the face of temptation, or loyalty to those he or she loves. A hero is an ultimate representation of what society wants from its best members, and the values of a particular moment in time are often quite clearly revealed by what kind of hero that time creates. Monsters and heroes speak to our personal psyches; we love to root for the good guy, and take guilty pleasure in the defeat of the bad guy. This is one of the deepest pleasures of mythology: Dreaming of being the great hero who is cheered on throughout history.

CHAPTER 12:
Human-Animal Hybrids: From Minotaur to Medusa

Human-animal hybrids exist in mythical and legendary tales throughout history. The ancient Romans had no monopoly on it: Think of our present fascination with werewolves and vampires—mainstay shapeshifters in popular culture. The mythological monsters that the Romans battled or befriended were, like much else in Roman mythology, derived from Greek sources. From the Minotaur to Medusa, these hybrid creatures were first described by the Greeks and embellished upon later by the Romans.

Why the fascination with human-animal hybrids? Psychologically speaking, it is fairly clear that these part-human, part-animal creatures represent our dual nature: On the one hand, we are all rational, thinking humans; on the other hand, we often nurture (and usually suppress) a wilder, more animalistic side. This wild side can be both fearsome and freeing. It can justify a desire to harm others with no more purpose, or it can allow us to dance in the moonlight and enjoy certain uncivilized delights. Animals are more closely aligned to nature, while humans are more closely aligned to culture. The portrayal of these hybrids vary, depending on how they are deployed in the particular mythical story they populate.

For one example, the legend of the Minotaur reverberates throughout Greco-Roman culture. The Minotaur is the half-man, half-bull offspring of a bestial affair, and, as such, is a monstrous abomination—a representation of uncivilized desire. King Minos of Crete was attempting to cement his somewhat-tenuous hold on power—his brothers also laid claim to the throne—and boasted that he could appeal to the gods, and they would grant him whatever he wanted, thus proving that he was divinely ordered to rule. He prayed fervently to Poseidon, the god of the sea, to produce the most magnificent bull ever seen, and Minos would promise to sacrifice it.

When the bull actually appeared, however, it was truly magnificent, and Minos wished to keep it for his own. So, he substituted another bull in sacrifice, thus angering the gods. There is a love spell placed on Pasiphae, Minos's wife, driving her to lust unnaturally after the bull Minos refused to sacrifice. In the Greek version of the story, it is Poseidon who casts this spell in order to assert his supremacy. In the Roman version of the story, however, it is Venus, the goddess of love, who so diabolically enchants Pasiphae, claiming that the woman had not shown proper piety to Venus. This highlights the cultural difference: The Roman emphasis on fidelity in marriage and propriety in women surely influenced the slight change in the story.

In both stories, Pasiphae is able to consummate her unnatural desire for the bull, and eventually gives birth to the Minotaur. Minos is horrified by the evidence of his wife's monstrous affair but does not, in fact, punish Pasiphae—perhaps realizing his own role in this betrayal. He hides the Minotaur away in the Labyrinth, and feeds it sacrificial subjects from the rival kingdom of Athens. The hero, Theseus, volunteers to serve as a tribute, and, so it was ordained, he was able to slaughter the hideous beast. Clearly, the myth serves several functions: First, it emphasizes obedience to the gods (Minos's error); second, it highlights the taboo against unnatural desire (Pasiphae's error); third, it provides a template for the creation of a new hero—Theseus. All heroes must prove themselves with great deeds, and the Minotaur was the occasion for Theseus.

Another monster common to Greco-Roman mythology is Medusa and her Gorgon sisters. There are several strands of the myth surrounding Medusa, with her famous hair of snakes and a stare that could turn men to stone. Many stories simply describe her and her two sisters as fierce Gorgons with the ability to kill men. One version of the story suggests that Medusa was once a beautiful maiden raped by Neptune in the temple of Minerva, who punished her (one wonders why) by turning her into a beast with snakes for hair and a serpent's tongue. Of the three sisters in the later telling, it was said that only Medusa was mortal. This provided, as the Minotaur did for Theseus, the stage for the creation of another hero, Perseus, who, using cleverness and strength—and, lest we not forget, help from the gods—ultimately kills her. He uses his shield as a mirror to see where Medusa is, instead of looking directly at her, and is able to cut off her head. This story is played out, over and over, in literary history, visual art, and popular culture.

There are friendly creatures in the world of human-animal hybrids, as well. The god Dionysius is often surrounded by satyrs—half-goat and half-man—who represent the spirit of drunken freedom seen at festival times. There are centaurs—half-horse and half-man—who are most often represented as civilized creatures with great wisdom that only bode ill if they become too drunk or too angry. These kinds of hybrids symbolize the cautionary tale that civilized humans can become less than such if they let their animal instincts take over, perhaps. Satyrs are friendly until their drunken desires cause them to assault maidens; centaurs are friendly until their anger leads to confrontation. Note that the animals associated with the fairly-friendly hybrids are goats and horses, which provide much use to humans, while the bull and snake hybrids are frightening and powerful.

CHAPTER 13:
Human-like Creatures: From Cyclops to the Sirens

Besides human-animal hybrids in Greek mythology, there are numerous characters who are human, or mostly human, but also have distinguishing features that set them apart. Like the hybrids, they are often personifications of the underlying fears of the people who tell these stories. Fears often reveal cultural prejudice and social anxiety better than almost anything else. From the frightening figure of the Cyclops to the seductive scariness of the Sirens, the Greeks revealed much about their world.

First, there are the Cyclops: These were creatures that were said to have risen, spontaneously, out of ancient Gaia, or Mother Earth. Some later accounts claim that they were actually the sons of Poseidon (there seem to be no actual accounts of female Cyclops—thus, they were a race doomed to die off). In any case, the Cyclops does not fit into any neat category created by Greek mythology: They are neither gods nor mortals, and neither Titans nor monsters. They are, quite simply, "Other."

Some legendary accounts of the Cyclops suggest that they have only one eye because they asked Zeus for the power to see the future. In exchange for one of their eyes, the wish was granted—but in a very twisted way. They were granted the ability to see the future, but only that of their own death.

Still, even as the Cyclops are maligned as threatening giants without a social conscience, they were utilized by the gods. At first, they are imprisoned in Tartarus because they are so hideous and uncivilized, but Cronus lets them out so that he can fight his child-eating father, Uranus. They are victorious, only to be banished back to Tartarus after their role in the overthrow. They are, again, released by Zeus in order to overthrow the Titans altogether, and again, they are successful. Zeus does not return them to Tartarus, and instead, as it is implied by some of the stories, gives them their own island. In thanks, the Cyclops is said to have given Zeus the gift of thunder and his signature lightning bolt—this begging the question of who, actually, wields more power.

The most famous of the Cyclops, Polyphemus, is, indeed, said to be the son of Poseidon, and it is he who drives along with the plot of *The Odyssey*. When Odysseus and his men land on the island of Cyclops on their way home from the Trojan War, they encounter Polyphemus. Actually, they come across his cave, invite themselves in, and proceed to eat his food and drink his wine. They wait for Polyphemus to return, with the intention of asking—demanding, more precisely—for more victuals to be given them for their continuing journey. But Polyphemus is none-too-pleased to see that the men have taken full advantage of his home without his consent. He proceeds to devour four of Odysseus' men and to shut them in his cave with an immovable boulder across the entrance: They are now hostages of Polyphemus, and fear that he will eventually devour them all.

Thanks to Odysseus' wily ways, they are able to escape: Odysseus gets the giant drunk, then pokes his one eye out with a sharpened pole. Blinded and bleeding, Polyphemus stumbles through his cave, shoving away the boulder to go outside and call for help—where he is also thwarted by Odysseus' cleverness (see Chapter 8). Odysseus and his men tie themselves to the bellies of Polyphemus' enormous sheep in order to evade capture (he may not be able to see them, but he can still smell and hear them). As they escape, Polyphemus roars out to his father, Poseidon, to have Odysseus killed. Because Odysseus was such a favorite of the gods—particularly the wise and ferocious Athena—Poseidon could not grant such extreme retribution; however, he promises to delay Odysseus' journey home by ten years. Thus, we get the masterwork that is *The Odyssey*.

Looking at the story through contemporary eyes, one can't help but have sympathy for the Cyclops. Used as pawns by the gods, they are banned from society—then expected to follow social rules: In the case of Polyphemus and Odysseus, they are both guilty of having broken one of the sacred rules of ancient, seafaring society—that of hospitality. In an age where travel was extraordinarily difficult, and communication between places virtually non-existent, it was simply expected that a host offers hospitality to a traveler, regardless of who they are or when they show up; Polyphemus does not conform to such a standard. As well, Odysseus breaks the rule by simply raiding the supplies of the Cyclops without being welcomed, and without following social convention. Thus, the story becomes more interesting for being more complex than simply "hero" versus "monster."

The Sirens are another version of the human-like creature with a complex provenance. While mostly human in the form of beautiful women, the Sirens were often described as having the wings (and sometimes body) of a bird. This makes them akin to the Harpies, another female-bird hybrid creature, whose shrill cries were the harbinger of death. The Sirens were also associated with fatality, but their methods were different.

The Sirens dwelt in the rugged cliffs of the islands in the Mediterranean, near where the sea monster Scylla and the ravaging whirlpool Charybdis lived. They would sing to sailors during the passage home, their voices so beautiful—and clearly enchanting, in the true sense of the word—that the sailors would go slightly mad and steer their ships directly into the rocks. Indeed, the cliffs upon which the Sirens dwelled were littered with the rotting carcasses and clean-picked bones of unlucky sailors.

The Sirens seem to represent both a fear of the natural world and a fear of feminine power. Certainly, the myth of Sirens luring sailors to their death is entirely appropriate in a society that constantly traveled through rough seas in primitive ships; many men were killed on their travels, and it would be comforting to have a story about what happened to them without implying that their seamanship was doubted. In addition, the Sirens belong to a long line of seductive women who are feared by men—this myth implies that men are helpless in the face of the magical power of women and must be forever vigilant, lest they fall victim to these devouring creatures. Again, with our contemporary eyes, we can see that the Sirens represent fear of the "Other," along with a fear of the natural world. These can serve us well in uncertain times, but can also reveal our cultural biases.

CHAPTER 14:
Perseus: Archetype of Heroism

The champion, Perseus, is one of the older heroes in Greek mythology, famed for his winged horse, Pegasus, and his role in rescuing the princess Andromeda—to say nothing of his infamous slaying of snake-headed Medusa. He was not only preternaturally strong, but he was also clever, and befriended by the gods. In addition to his own prowess, he was given a magical helmet that allowed him to be invisible, and a pair of winged sandals which allowed him a kind of flight. He was popular throughout the Greek islands and beyond, representing a clear heroic ideal.

As with many of the heroes in ancient Greek mythology, Perseus claimed divine parentage. His mother, Danae, was imprisoned in a basement made of pure bronze, which was supposed to keep out any suitor. Her father, King Akrisios, had heard of a prophecy that one day, a grandson would kill him, so he intended to keep Danae prisoner. Still, a cell made of bronze was no match for Zeus, who presented himself in a shower of golden rain, and laid with Danae. When the child Perseus was born, Akrisios took no chances, and locked mother and child in a chest and had them thrown out to sea. Zeus did not abandon them entirely, and saw them wash up safely onto the shores of Seriphos, where Perseus grew up unmolested.

While he grew into a strong young man, the king of the island began to have designs on his mother, Danae, and he wanted Perseus out of the way. So, he hatched the plan to have Perseus—who had boasted of his great abilities—kill the Gorgon, Medusa; a task deemed impossible for any man. Not only did she have snakes for hair, but her very gaze turned men into stone. Nevertheless, Perseus was another favorite of the gods, and got help from Hermes and Athena. They told him to seek counsel from the wise—if wicked—witches, sisters of Medusa. Perseus wanted to know where Medusa dwelled, and he wanted some magical gifts to help him dispatch her. These witches wouldn't give information willingly, of course, but they did have a weakness: They shared one eye. So, through cunning trickery, Perseus managed to steal their one eye and threatened to keep it, should they not give him information. In some versions, they tell him how to obtain the cap of Hermes, which renders the wearer invisible, and winged sandals to help him fly. In other versions, Athena gives Perseus a shield, which he uses to deflect Medusa's gaze.

In any case, Perseus found Medusa, and either wearing the cap of invisibility or deflecting her gaze with the shield, was able to cut off her head. However, the head of Medusa didn't simply die; like a snake, it writhed on, and her gaze still had the power to turn men to stone. Perseus had also requested a magical sack in which to put the head so that he would be protected. Keeping the head may seem strange, but imagine what a powerful weapon it could be—and, indeed, was.

On his triumphant journey home, Perseus came upon the beautiful princess Andromeda. She was chained to a rock to be sacrificed to Poseidon's terrible sea monster (In Greek, *ketos*, though in recent popular culture, the creature is called the "Kraken"). Her mother, Cassiopeia, had boasted that she was more beautiful than even Poseidon's sea nymphs, the Nereids, and Poseidon demanded appeasement. In an extreme moment of "love at first sight," Perseus offers to deal with the beast in exchange for Andromeda's hand in marriage. The frightened king agrees, and Perseus uses his secret weapon: The head of Medusa. He turns the sea monster to stone and is granted his wish to be married to Andromeda. Another suitor gets in his way, claiming he had already been promised her hand, so Perseus simply shows him Medusa and turns him to stone, too.

When he returns home, he learns that Akrisios had sent him on this journey in order to take advantage of his mother, and had been treating her poorly. So when he presented the head of Medusa to the king, he had his gaze into her eyes, and—poof!—he is turned to stone, as well. Eventually, Perseus presents Athena with her head (Medusa was the creation of Athena in the first place) who gives it pride of place in her ethereal palace.

Later, Perseus' exploits are perhaps less well-known, but he did fulfill the original prophecy and killed his grandfather—accidentally, as it turns out, at a sporting contest. Because of his unpleasant memories of home, he decides to leave and found his own kingdom in Mycenae, marking him in the hall of other founding heroes, Hercules and Theseus, and later, the Latin Aeneas.

CHAPTER 15:
Theseus: Founder of Athens

As with Perseus, Theseus is an archetypal hero and city-state founder. Through his many brave deeds, adventurous exploits, and clever mind, he came to represent the ideal Athenian: A man of action who was also just and smart—a defender of the first democracy. His most famous exploit was the killing of the ferocious Minotaur of the Cretan legend. His most lasting legacy was the glory of Athens during the classical age of ancient Greece.

Like Perseus (and other heroes), Theseus had divine origins. His father was said to be the son of Poseidon—or King Aegeus of Athens—and his background was kept secret to him until he came of age. In the myth of his coming of age, his father left him a gift of sandals and a sword buried under a rock at the shoreline. When he was strong enough to lift the rock, he could then retrieve his gifts. Once he did, he set out to Athens to claim his inheritance.

Along the way, as is appropriate for a hero, he must prove himself through many confrontations and obstacles. First, he dispatched a couple of villains— thugs or highway robbers who terrorized travelers— and was able to secure another weapon for himself in the process: A mighty iron club. Next, he had to best the evil Skiron, who blocked the sea passage by tricking travelers into washing their feet and, when bent over, were shoved off the cliff to be dashed on the rocks below. Theseus was too clever to fall for this, and instead, subjected Skiron to his own unjust punishment.

Then, he encountered the brutish wrestler, Kerkyon, who crushed his opponents to death. Of course, Theseus was no ordinary opponent, and bested Kerkyon at his own game. Finally, he dealt with Procrustes, a villainous trickster who offered travelers respite, only to maim them with his exacting standards: If a traveler was too long for his bed, he would hack off their limbs as they dangled over; if a traveler was too short for his bed, he would chain and stretch him to the length of the bed. Theseus quickly got rid of him by tricking him into getting into bed, then subjecting him, yet again, to his own brutal punishment. Theseus was also instrumental in the hunting down and dispatching of many animal creatures, too, who were considered beyond the reach of ordinary men.

His most famous exploit took place after his arrival in Athens. The city had been compelled to send, each year, seven men and seven women to Crete to feed the terrible Minotaur. This was retribution for the killing of the Cretan champion and king's son after he surprisingly won the Athens games. Theseus wanted to put an end to this practice, so he nobly volunteered to be one of the tributes.

Along the way to Crete, Theseus was given a magic ring that supposedly made him fearless, as the half-man, half-bull Minotaur was a terrible creature, indeed. Thus, he entered the Labyrinth in which the monster was held with confidence to spare; nobody had ever emerged from the Labyrinth once they entered it. Theseus, using his cleverness as well as his strength, unwound a ball of string while chasing the Minotaur through the tricky Labyrinth. He was able to slay the beast, then find his way out by following his unspooled roll of string. His heroism and fame were thus cemented.

Returning to Athens, he inadvertently caused tragedy when he forgot to fly the white flag on his ship, signaling to his king (and possibly father) that he was alive. The black sail, instead, was up, and the king thought that Theseus had been killed. In his despair, he flung himself from the castle into the sea (this is where the Aegean Sea allegedly gets its name). Saddened, Theseus nonetheless was free to take the throne and reign with justice and virtue for many years to come. Understandably, the myth of Theseus gained much prominence during the classical age of Greece when Athens was its most powerful city-state.

Chapter 16: Other Enchanting Stories & Figures

As one can easily imagine, this set of stories has merely scratched the surface of what's available in the canon of Greek myths and legends. Remember that the Greek peoples eventually covered a vast area and developed a highly sophisticated set of societies, so there are innumerable legends and tales about innumerable gods and heroes, goddesses and enchantresses, monsters and foes. Roman mythology also clearly reverberates even today, as we have seen throughout, influencing popular culture in many ways—large and small.

There are so many myths within the Greco-Roman canon that it would be difficult to recount them all in one place. Some other enchanting stories that one could further investigate include the following:

The myth of the Amazons was a legendary race of warrior women who lived separately from the world of men. Of course, we know of the Amazons through the singular figure of Diana Prince, or Wonder Woman. From the old DC Comics to the 1970s campy television show, to the recent blockbuster hit, Wonder Woman has created a myth of Amazonian proportions for contemporary times.

Pandora was the first mortal woman, created by Zeus, in a competition with Poseidon. She was sent down to Earth with her lovely box, expressly forbidden to open it. Of course, she proved quite the mortal and, too tempted by the forbidden, she opened Pandora's Box, thus releasing all the ills—such as plague, famine, and war—into the mortal world.

Eros and Psyche were the god of love and the goddess of the soul, respectively. Their union represented the culmination of Greek social and philosophical ideas of combining (and taming) passion with a purified soul. Plato's tripartite soul surely borrows some ideas from this ancient myth.

Apollo and Daphne also represent a Greek romantic ideal. The beautiful god Apollo longs for the beautiful nymph, Daphne, but she does not reciprocate his advances. In fact, she wished to be turned into a tree so that Apollo could not seduce her. Thus, their non-union is considered the template for what we now call "platonic" love—that is, love purified of passion.

The Greeks often used myths to explain or elaborate—even to beautify and elevate—a natural phenomenon. The story of Callisto is that of a young girl who is seduced by Zeus and becomes pregnant, angering her benefactor, the (virgin) goddess Artemis, who turns Callisto into a bear. Her son was fated to kill her, but Zeus intervened. Before the boy could throw his spear into the bear that used to be his mother, Zeus turned them both into stars—hence, we have the constellations Ursa Major and Ursa Minor (*Ursa* means "bear"), or the Big Dipper and the Little Dipper. We still gaze upon the constellations created via Greek mythology thousands of years ago (Cassiopeia, Orion the Hunter, and the zodiac signs), which turn the mysterious night sky into something delightful.

Other popular cultural references to ancient Greece include the hit series *Percy Jackson and The Olympians* by Rick Riordan. These books, for young adults, but fun for any age, follow the adventures of Percy (you know, short for "Perseus"), who we learn is a demi-god, the son of Poseidon. He goes away to Camp Half-Blood to learn how to be a hero, and makes some friends and some notorious enemies, all while speaking the language of a modern teenager. All of the famous Greek myths are somehow woven into the books with an amusing contemporary twist. If you saw the regrettable movie version, be aware that the books are a compelling read and delicious fun.

There are also the *300* films, glamorizing the Spartan battle state while demonizing the Persians. These are definitely for an older audience and should be viewed with a skeptical eye, as entertaining as they may be. Finally, the tale of Perseus and Andromeda is told, including Medusa and the Kraken, in the original *Clash of the Titans* (1981) and in the 2010 remake. The original Claymation animation certainly looks old-fashioned to us now, but it's still an enjoyable romp.

Conclusion

There is nothing quite like the power of myth to move us to think about other peoples and other places. The legendary feats of heroes, the dastardly deeds of monsters and sometimes gods, and the sweeping scope of epic tales, all draw us into a different world. Myths serve a crucial purpose: They function to remind us of who we are, and how we should (and should *not*) behave. They also explain the world to peoples before the advent of science and technology, creating comfort in times of strife and scarcity.

Greek mythology is unique, in that the peoples who created these tales and the practitioners of the attending religious beliefs were also the peoples who were a part of the most influential culture in the West, spreading ideas on democracy, philosophy, and mythology throughout the world and also Western history. Thus, Greek mythology is bound by certain motifs—the significance of the city-state; the inherent human quality in all beings, supernatural or not; the importance of territory and reputation—that appear throughout the canon. Ancient Greek mythology was not, unlike other older mythologies, significantly impacted by merging with other cultures and/or belief systems; in fact, the Romans adopted most of Greek mythology, wholesale, ensuring the continuation of this marvelous canon. In addition, this older material—obscured during the dark and Middle Ages—was rediscovered during the Renaissance period, and resurrected, mostly intact, serving as a reminder for a different way of life. This serves to highlight the grandeur of Greek mythology and its truly epic scope; hence, it's continuing widespread appeal.

Hopefully, as you reach the end of your journey here, you take up new roads to learn more about the other traditions and tales mentioned throughout. As new tellings of ancient Greek culture and mythology have captivated our popular imagination, so should the original tales likewise demand our fascination.

Connect with us on our Facebook page
www.facebook.com/bluesourceandfriends and stay
tuned to our latest book promotions and free
giveaways.